MW00477916

Myths Unheard

Ashlee Depass

BookLeaf
Publishing

Presentation by *BookLeaf Publishing*

Web: www.bookleafpub.com

E-mail: info@bookleafpub.com

ISBN: 9789357744850

First edition 2023

To those who knew I could, especially my family.

PREFACE

"What happens when gods forget how to love?
When they become so tired of caring
about us mortals and our grain sized lives?

Do they lose regard for our safety entirely?
Do they start playing with our fates
the way children play dolls?

Do they just stop protecting our ever fleeting
mortality?
Do they become mortal themselves?

What happens to the gods with mortally
induced heartbreaks?
Does a small piece of them,
just die?"

Legends Get Twisted

Cowards turn to heroes
With a simple change of song–

Now if the Speaker tells the tale wrong,
Can you truly blame the world–
If the public remembers
The story wrong

Mortality is fatal,
This we know for sure–
Good or bad:

It is determined
Not by truth–
bu rather it is decided by:

Who wins and who survives

Echo is Born

When every word you speak is ignored or
misconstrued
You learn to stop speaking lest spoken to
And gradually I was spoken to less.
When I had tried to speak mind,
The words fell on deaf ears–
Yet when it came to their beckoning,
Of course I called back
And all of a sudden,
All ears seemed to have fun, and listen.

What was a new plaything to them
was my voice lost to the wind.

Silence is…

I've heard silence described as magical
 Like the best party trick is leaving a room
speechless.
 A miracle only mankind may grant without
divine intervention.
 A gift that keeps on giving.

 But I've never known quiet that isn't
deafening–
 That doesn't cause my heart to reach for drums
in my ears,
 Leaving my chest.

 The only silence i've known wasn't peaceful
 Or sweet like fresh honey off the comb.
 Silence has never been sweet or kind to me.

 Silence is the buzzing of a bee–
 Incessant and anxious to sting first.
 It is the dead of night–
 The cricket that does not chirp in the dead of
night.
 It is the danger that sits ever present

 –With deep breaths and perked ears–

Which preys on the cricket in the dead of night.
It is the death of the cricket that tried to play a
merry tune.

It is the moment before the other foot drops–
A game of chicken–
A bloody war that leaves no proof of its
existence
Except for the coat of awkwardness it brings to
hangs up at your door– or throw across your
floor–
or drop on the side of a bed where a life sleeps
no more.

It is a give and give relationship with a
blackhole.
It takes and takes until you have no more–
It is giving all of you till there's nothing left.
It is the nothing left.

–The lump that forms in the back of your
throat–
It chokes you out–
It is all that is left dead and unsaid.

Silence is the nothing.
The pin dropping into your finger
As you swat away the buzzing bee–

Anxious but unaware of the danger lurking
outside–
Waiting to hang its coat– right on your front
door step.
Silence is the death of the cricket you didn't
hear–

Silence is the nothing left
–never peaceful–
It is the absence of a heart beat–
and often is followed by the stench of death.

Hades

I am judged by all
In each new rendition
Of a tale I never got to tell.

Painted as a villain in their narratives
But has anyone ever questioned the source?
Have they ever provided me enough benefit of
the doubt
To listen to my version of the story?

How often have I truly hurt them
To deserve how often they hurt me?

Don't they know?
I am so much more than the titles
That have been given to me.

Aphrodite

Born from a raging sea and blood,
 Beauty and love incarnate
 Her looks are a weapon in their own right
 And boy, does she know how to use them.
 She could bring War to his knees,
  Begging for mercy.
 And despite all the ways she will break you
 You'll still thank her for the experience later.

 She knows love is a necessity
 upon which civilizations have
 Been created and destroyed to keep.
 Don't underestimate her
 She knew what she was doing,
  when she started the trojan war
  and came out of it blameless.

Silence Hurts

Silence choked out my pride.
Never feeling comfortable in my mouth
—Wordless spaces have always felt foreign.—
To hear a pin drop terrifies me.

—Like a tumor in the back of my throat—
Quiet is as unnatural to me as purple skin.
Incurable and insatiable in its hunger—
It is desperate to swallow me whole.

I feel no peace in the dead of night
if I can't at least hear the crickets sing—
Awkward pauses and vehement secrecy
Leave me shifting in my seat

—My ears prick up any time I can hear the
wind howl—
The torture of not knowing what to say,
or what is about to be said
I learned to read into the stillness of every
peaceful moment.

Like the calm before the storm,
I brace myself for the other shoe to drop

The words start to tumble and fumble over
themselves
 as I scramble to fill the void that threatens to
suck me in

Death's Ferryman

Liberty is in death
The way payment is in life.

We assume
the one who guides us through our deaths
Stands, waiting at his boat–
His hand– expectantly open–
Waiting for compensation.

Yet what does mortality need money for?
It is only man that pays to live
And so it is only man who can imagine
They must also pay for rest in their death.

Yet death for all it costs the living,
Has always seemed to be:
The cheapest cost
In any currency

Echo I

That was all that was left.

Just an image of someone else bouncing off her
rough edges.

She'd become no more than a whisper,

A shade

A parrot to be mocked

Lost to the wind

Tell me if a tree falls and there is no one around
to prove it,
How could it ever make a sound?

Only in silence could she hear herself.

Persephone

My lover kills.
 He kills himself
 Slaving away to his empire of Shades.

My lover kills.
Kills me.
Buries me six feet under,
Right along side himself.
He dawns a crown of cold hard gold,
As i wear my own, made of thorns,
For that's all that seems to thrive.

He kills me,
By killing himself.
Our subjects as dead as he,
Despite our immortality.

Back home I am mourned,
By a mother left in abandon
(for his false promises)
She claims I'm already dead–
Dead to her anyway.

My lover kills.
He can't help it.

He kills all that I grow,
With just a touch—
I'm left drunk off my own rotten vines
Attempting to forget the stench of death,
That surrounds us.

Eros is Not so Innocent

Do you truly believe him to be all flowers and
chocolate sweets?

He has always been a marksman,
with a killer's precision
He stalks his prey in every place
no one would expect to find him.

He feels no remorse as he lets loose each arrow.
A hunter starving for the thrill of the case.
He saviors in the aiming of his bow,
—Loaded— negligent of the power he wields.

Each of his victims selected at random.
There is no mercy, no pity in his heart.

Fathered by war and lust.
Born out the chaos
of bloodlust and desire.
He was conceived from passionate impulse
and a blatant disregard for others.

He is the child of love and war
And has never played by the rules
Of either.

He's never cared if love is required or not.
Instead he has found joy in making people fall
And fall hard—
Whether it be on the dance floor or the battle
grounds,
Where he lets loose has never meant anything to
him before.

Still we foolishly believe there is any rhyme to
his reason.
That there must be a method to the madness.
To think destiny or free will has any say in the
matter is foolish.
We convince ourselves he is malevolent.
We believe him merciful,
To be the best of love and lust.

All the while we forget
There has never been anything fair in love or
war.
Love has always been blood thirsty and touch
starved

Prometheus

Why do you run?

I run for fear that if i don't flee now,
I shall never know
Just why the smell of smoke in my lungs
Has never been foreign.

How did I Start the fire?

The truth:
I didn't.
One day i just noticed how my heart seemed
aglow
And my stomach felt like a pig on a spit,
Turning 'round and 'round as night bore on dark,
Starving for what I'd justly earned and
sought for myself.

Why did you run?

You were a blanket.
Stifling, suffocating, difficult to stay under.
I knew you'd only put my flames out.
Force me to rely on your temporary warmth
So that i may depend on you,

In all the ways i promised myself not to.

How did you start the fire?

I didn't start the fire!
The fire started in me,
And with it I ran
To give all the i had and all that i knew
To those below
Who were as despare for the light
As I used to be.

Hypnos

Why do you never come to me when i need you.
 You leave me waiting till the clock strikes three
every night
 And still I stay up each night patiently and
pained
 Counting the seconds, minutes, hours
 Until you peek in through the door and envelop
me.
 You always feel like the sweetest dreams.

 Yet I lie awake each night,
 Knowing you won't come through the door till
its too late,
 Drunk on the night life
 And ignorant of the suffering you inflict.
 Ignorant of my fear that one night
 I may never see you again.

Erebus Wishes for a New Domain

No one knows it but
 I crave to be the sun–
Lighting up every space i enter,
My smile beaming across rooms
And skys all day.
My presence alone
able to brighten even the darkest of nights.

But there is something stopping me.
It feels like ants crawling all over
'Till it envelops me.
It wisks me into the shade,
The shadows–my home– devour me.

Like a candle snuffed out,
before it even gets to burn.
With nothing more than a short breath,
Day turns to a starless night around me.

Free is not a word in my vocabulary.
Trapped in a glass coffin, inside a dark box–
There's no oxygen to breathe–
I have nothing to ignite the restless heart inside
me.

I suffocate on my own silence.
My lungs stop functioning
for 3 seconds, 2 eternities,
and it all happens in the span of 1 moment
too long.

What else can a fire do with nothing to feed it
And nowhere to go,
But die, slowly but surely.
Tell me if a candle is snuffed out by the wind
In the middle of a forest, with no one around–
Was it ever really lit?
Or was it just a random and lonely
Little wick?

Hyacinth

Oh how the sunny days melted my woes away.

Playing catch with love and laughing with him too.

There was no brighter times than when I could be in his sweltering embrace.

But the winds of change always come.

Sweet summer days must end someday, someway.

And who would've suspected jealousy cold as ice

—Like snow down your spine—

You could feel the air shift and twirl like harbinger flapping its wings.

Oh cruel Zephyrus,

if not for you my fun under the sun would have been sweet eternal joy

But now I lie in the ground, forced to take root just to survive,

This infinitely lonely winter, for the rest of my life.

Psyche

When the people you love
 Keep you in the dark,
 You learn to love with the lights out,
 Learn to see in the night
 As if it were day
 And it becomes ever so difficult for you
 To finally let the midnight oil burn
 In fear the glow of the flames
 Will give you a migraine.

 The seems to blind you
 And its rays seem to burn.
 But i promise you,
 Once you let in the light

 Even Cupid won't be able to convince to come
back into the darkness you never should have
had to stumble through.

Icarus

I was told to stay away from from the sun
because I'd only get burned.

I never was the type to listen though..

Instead, I fell and laughed as my wax wings
cooked my bare back

(The waves below were prepared to catch me as
I crashed into them).

I knew what i was doing would hurt but i did it
anyway.

And as the last few feathers fell from my back,
The wax melting away as a I laughed

And the sun — He laughed back

And with that I felt the spark of inspiration as I
fell to my fate.

I finally understood the price the artist pays for
talent and passion,

For they are the ones who touch the sun

And it is basic knowledge that if you touch
something with passion like fire

You are bound to get burned.

I opened my arms to the sun and for a moment I
felt his embrace return mine.

Echo II

He never truly loved me, just the idea.
 The lie I made just for him.
 The kind that imitated his every like and
opinion.
 Like a reflection of the mind;
 I replicated him so well I supposed he thought
my voice was his own.
 Perhaps that's why,
 despite all the love I had in my heart
 I could not bring my own voice to speak on it,
 Silently
 I watched him fall in love with someone
 Much more similar to him than me

Hestia

Forgotten girl.
 Homebody through and through.
 The mediator that gets overlooked.
 You're the one who's going to make this family
work
 Even if it kills you.

 Your heart is so big
 And despite how no one seems to remember
your name
 You are the the flame that keeps this home
warm.

Penelope

I come undone each night
 As you stay out late,
 I wonder if you'll make it home alive.

My heart is pure and arrow true,
It only leads me back to you but..
Your mind's crazy for an odyssey,
Adventure and fame like a siren's call
Pull you away from me.
But I'll wait an eternity for you

I'd fight off whirl pools and monsters too.
 So why is it you forget me so quickly if I'm not
lying next to you.
 You've found yourself bewitched by witches
 and charmed by enchantresses,
 But you claimed they never held any power
over you.

You left a cold spot
 in out mighty oak bed (blessed by marriage)
 And slept in the warmth of another
 While I've remained alone
 in a race for you to get home
 Before our family falls.

No matter how hard i try,
I can't seem to forget your smile.
The way you hold me,
Makes me feel like royalty.

Orion

It seems to me the worst torcher is
 To be among the stars
 If I cannot be by your side dear Moon.

 Like Cupid you struck me arrow true
 Without so much of clue
 And now I can find no brighter light
 Than your smile,
 Full and bright
 As it should be for a goddess like you.

 So how sick must the fates have been
 To have us destine to be a part of the same
world
 Yet so very, very far apart.

Atlas

I hold the world on my back,
 Bearing the weight of it all
 On brittle bones and immobile muscles.
 But a crack, a break a mistake,
 They are luxuries in which i cannot partake in.

 So it doesn't matter, come rain, sleet, hail, or
snow,
 It doesn't matter if I'm about to collapse
 The world keeps spinning
 And I'm just left stagnant,
 Smiling through the storm clouds
 that swirl around my eyes
 All the time.